OLD HORSE,
WHAT IS TO BE DONE?

OLD HORSE,
WHAT IS TO BE DONE?

poems by

STEPHEN KUUSISTO

TIGER BARK PRESS ❀ ROCHESTER, NEW YORK ❀ 2020

Published by Tiger Bark Press,
202 Mildorf Ave., Rochester, NY 14609.

Tiger Bark Press books are published by Steven Huff,
and designed by Philip Memmer.

Cover photo by Michael Meteyer.
Author photo by Connie Kuusisto.

ISBN-13: 978-1-7329012-6-1

SECOND PRINTING

Publication of this book made possible with public funds from the New York State Council on the Arts with the support of Governor Andrew M. Cuomo and the New York State Legislature.

Contents

One

You'll Have to Take My Word	11
Thinking of Ted Berrigan	12
The Writing Prompt	13
Remembering Donald Justice	15
1919	16
Fall Arrives in the Finger Lakes	17
Notes on a Christmas Morning	19
A Hand	21

Two

The Half-Finished Garden	25
It Is Early or Late for Different People	26
Aubade	28
Sand	29
Carnivale	30
Praxis: Deliberate Beauty	33
Autumn, or Rain	39
Notebook, October 2017	41
A Vague Love for Parsifal	45
Notebook Elegy for Pentti Saarikoksi	49
Travelogue	50
Horse, Man, Helsinki	51
A Brief Poem Written at the End of a Bitter Year	52
Homage to James Tate	53
God at Home	54
Micro Memoir 68	55
Conditions	56
The Uproar of Living by Day…	57
Counting on My Fingers	58

Three

Elegy	61
Old Horse, What Is to Be Done?	62
Frost on Windowpanes	63
Larch, I'm Going Sad Like a Toy…	64
Meadow	65
Per Caputque Pedesqu…	66
Underneath the Willow	67
Blind, I Bought a Horse	68
Hymn	69
Late in the Day	70
Like a Falling Leaf	71
At the Arts Center	72
Rain in a Tin Dish	73
Late	74
Ode	75
Alone in Any City	76
Dear Jarkko	77
Emergent God	78
A Brief Essay on Romanticism	79
After So Much is Said	80
Lorca	81
To a Blind Man Selling Pencils	82
Questions to Answers	83
Raven, Helsinki Harbor	84
Leafage	85
Ode to the Future Perfect	87
Empty Paths	88
Ripeness is All	90
Acknowledgements	93
About the Author	95
Colophon	97

For Robert Bly

*I am proud only of those days that pass in
undivided tenderness.*

PART ONE

Rebellion simply makes a man old...

—*Jarkko Laine*

You'll have to take my word...

I've outgrown sentiment like the old apples
On old trees—spirit quiet
Clean with decline.
As a boy I was loud
With rebellions,
Buying birds
For instance, releasing them
In parking lots
Where the grilles of Chevrolets
Gleamed in heartbreak.
It's understatement to say I'm tired.
Leave a message, I'll be in touch.
The oldest apples hang far into autumn,
Glow against bare limbs
As if Aphrodite has passed,
Preoccupied as she must be.

Thinking of Ted Berrigan on the Day of First Snow

For my sins I lived in Iowa City and my heart was dark as poetry itself—
My little heart, my raven, my common bird of dispositions,
Joyful that God is no God to the hearts, birds, poems. The nest box
Of hearts, birds, poems sways up in the ash tree.
The hearts, birds, poems make a place in all weather.
See Picasso: "A person, an object, a circle
Are all 'figures'; they react on us more or less intensely..."
Ted, no gods but walking lightly with tiny silver bells today...

The Writing Prompt

for Doug Anderson

Think about the pressure that makes each fact float,
High rise buildings at the edge of_____,
In my case, Helsinki, the apartment complexes
"Post-war" vaguely Stalinist, "a good place
For electro-shock" and the architect
Now in a mad house. 4A stands where
Once, in '38, they made machine guns
And a row of bicycles waits
Like old horses queuing for hay,
Children pitch coins at the bus stop,
Flickering faces share structural damage
From repeated loading—half the locals
Have turned to stones or worse.
My trick was to rise early,
Walk out "into" one of those photos
From the last century,
Forget the hell of nothing
And show off my brand new suit
To a circle of crows.
I was young back then
And used to think about two truths approaching,
Money and labor, music and envy,
Tautological, drunk,
Seeing stains through the wallpaper,
Blind of course, pushed across streets
by strangers, what a muddle!
Think about the pressure that makes each fact float.
Think about the invisible ink devised

By George Washington and remember
Despite this caution, our first president
Also wrote in code.

Remembering Donald Justice

And so what does it mean, pale geographies of the heart,
The wishful hour alone at a window?
Boyhood:
Blind with puppets and homemade songs.

Will the hours ever be softer than in those days?
It was sweet to be lost with the crickets.

1919

Now the children have climbed into the trees though it's winter. Look at them, they are both preoccupied and disinterested.

{Marginalia} True: the poet hasn't shown the children. Accordingly you have only propositions. The children high in the snowy branches look like scientists or aesthetes. But are they boys and girls? Girls only?

{Marginalia} The poet is filled with ideas but stingy.

So the poet goes back to work: the year, 1919. Finland. Starvation. The children were sent into the branches since the elders believed air was cleaner up there. The adults imagined influenza was down by the roots.

{Marginalia} Images make poems, facts make life. One little girl in a tall birch had such impudent beautiful eyes. Eyes blue-going-to-gray. "Wisdom eyes" her grandfather called them.

Fall Arrives in the Finger Lakes

The poets always say "if"
The mosquitoes say "now"
Exchange is a puzzle

**

Up river empty houses
Lean in the wind

**

When writing
Add footnotes—
George Washington
Spilled blood over there

**

By those birches
People tried in vain
To silence anxiety

**

Tattered maple tree
Squandering light

**

The summer has been dark as a bed

**

The poets always say "if"
As in: if the soul gets loose

**

When I close my eyes
I see Winter's mask:
Gold leaves

Notes on Christmas Morning

Those houses in Iceland like boats half buried
And their prows pointing to heaven

**

We were driving aimlessly
I was carrying on about Snorri Sturluson
My friend Gary wanted a good cigar

**

Saarikoski: "We were simply too simple.
Time went by, men and women, bellies and bird song.
We came to be old, we fluttered, that's all."

**

Wind in the chimney flue
Sun not up yet
Saarikoski: "The canaries on their way to the Faeroe Islands are lurking
    in their pleasures."

**

When I was young I complained about everything
E. Power Biggs on the radio
Gramophone shards in my boots

**

Ice covered the pond like an illness
I was sad in my twenties
Sometimes I read the right things
Silly old Kalevala and John Donne

**

I love Pasolini's *Gospel According to St. Matthew*
I would also like to be a Catholic-Marxist

**

Thoughts and poems circulate
I love the Jesus who lets me stay blind

A Hand

After Jane Hirshfield:
"A hand is not four fingers and a thumb."

I say it's a horse grazing in tall grass.
I say it's the ligaments of twilight.
I agree it's a transparent question.
There is a hand inside the hand
Like the story in a tree.
The hand in the mind is smooth.
There are the hands of Bartholomew
Heavy or light in season.
Hands of the autumn rain.
Taking bread; taking up green;
The last out of this bowl;
Scripture of the moon.

PART TWO

An ancient man came to meet me on the riverbank,
with a broken thread in his wrist.
Moonlight shimmered through him and through his entrails,
his heart pulsed like a lampwick.
He laid his old hand on my head:
The boat's waiting,
no need for oars, or a wind.

—Eeva Liisa Manner

The Half-Finished Garden

Oh I could kiss you Transtromer—
Darkness against my face
Your Haydn, not mine, playing
Underfoot... Piano
For native country—

Up late walking the dogs with my dead father in mind...
How does it go?

It is Early or Late for Different People

It's a Mozart morning—not all of them are—
There's Suor Angelica or Gillespie, Dizzy; Caruso; even Peer Gynt.
But this is a dawn for Piano Concerto #23 in A, K 488,
Its second movement breaking my heart the way it did when I was a boy.

Dangle a heart—there's flying in our lives. Drop it like a sucking wave—
there's so much sorrow. A little boy with bandages on his eyes listens be-
side a record player, a late summer's day…

**

How early did he know himself? Very. Don't you understand what Mozart
does?

**

It's the adagio kills me.

**

It is late or early for different people
I am without a name
Others talk in the smoky railway car
Morning sun—the loneliest physics—
My feet shift under the seat
As though my toes
Stitch seams on carpet
How one makes poems from nothing—
A train, a few flickering points—
Don't cry body, we're going someplace

**

Finnish poet Tua Forsstrom: "Nothing terrifies us more than the godforsaken places…"

I don't know about this.

When I think about it—terror and nothing sacred, I think less of the outer world and more about my bones.

She would say: godforsaken means bones too… not just ruined orchards…

But the bones invented godforsaken in their private sphere.

**

Well well
I didn't have much when I came
Don't have much now
I do have a well-worn record of "Swan Lake"

**

I like black currants…

Aubade

Finally at 60 I see there's no science to the self,
Freud sails in his Viking boat, circling

The Aland Islands, where once, when young
I made love with a girl atop a grave.

We smoked later, naked
Beneath pointillist summer stars,

Believing we were chaff
Waiting to be gods.

Sand

I woke to the waves and sand and realized I'd been dreaming of my father.
We were in Finland back in the late fifties, a time when it seemed people
didn't laugh. The water had to do all the laughing in those days. Clouds
watched the children. There were very few televisions. I remember the
adults reading books by the sea. The ocean was everyone's philosopher.
Those were beautiful days. Everyone had their cup of sand.

Carnivale

Beyond countenance is a simplicity born of color. It is politically incorrect nowadays to talk of madmen, but at sunset the mad are either speechless or very talkative. What else? All the buildings in town appear on fire.

I told you this long before.

The soul becomes dyed with the color of its thoughts. Marcus Aurelius stood in a marsh and tracked ribbons of light on the water's surface. I suppose he did this because Aristotle did also. The motives of colorists are pure suppositions.

With color one obtains an energy that seems to stem from witchcraft. Henri Matisse performed a seance under his hat.

"Reason is negative and dialectical, because it resolves the determinations of the understanding into nothing." (Hegel) Color is more of nothing. Color rides zero in and out of the windows.

I saw this when young. I thought the window was a place. My nose against frosted glass. The self-construing eye and its tints. Adults murmuring in the next room.

"There is nothing, nothing in heaven, or in nature or in mind or anywhere else which does not equally contain both immediacy and mediation." (Hegel again) You see, even Hegel was a colorist.

Einstein: "*Fantasie ist wichtiger als Wissen.*" ("Imagination is more important than knowledge.") Color is the siphon. I know a man who plays a red piano. "Art is what you can get away with." (Warhol) The best time to play a red piano is dusk. "Color... thinks by itself, independently of the object it clothes." (Baudelaire)

So you stand up. Drunk because your eyes are bad. Monet threw away his eyeglasses. What is that? It is a purple hibiscus. Someone not you planted it. "Color is an act of reason." (Bonnard) The most rational mind in the world put this flower here. She was rational as a fox.

Raw Umber, Cadmium Red Light, Burnt Umber. Climbing stairs. Perfect tiny attic windows.

"We were always intoxicated with color, with words that speak of color, and with the sun that makes colors live." (Andre Derain)

"A thimbleful of red is redder than a bucketful." (Matisse)

"Colors are both of us: the fool and the pragmatist. When I haven't any blue I use red." (Picasso)

Once when I was a small boy and sailing to Europe with my parents the steward set fire to a dish of crepes. I was overjoyed and simultaneously heart broken. All that blue I couldn't touch...and the delight of strangers...

The problem for colorists: they can't tell a proper story. Color flies like leaves in wind.

Hans Hofmann: "Color is a plastic means of creating intervals... color harmonics produced by special relationships, or tensions. We differentiate Now between formal tensions and color tensions, just as we differentiate In music between counterpoint and harmony."

"Everything is ceremony in the wild garden of childhood." (Neruda)

I crawled under dark pines as a child, searching for the northern orchid known as the Lady's Slipper. One could find it because it was the color of royalty.

Formal tensions and color tensions, the iridescent orchid of the subconscious. I never got over it.

I recognize I've already told you this.

The years of my childhood trembled, the hours were green. I lay in the garden in the wet light of summer and listened to the songs of rhubarb and thistles.

Immediacy and mediation: I believed colors would come to know me.

I have no reason to change my view.

At sundown I feel talkative. Dawn was a time of silence. The colors are not the same.

Inside the sunset there is a sunset, its ceremony formal in two traditions: One of hypothesis and the other of history.

Praxis: Deliberate Beauty

It's a hard life and art won't help you live.

Words are occasionally lethal.

Language is a trick. God knows.

**

(From a notebook:

In a few minutes I will land in Ashgabat which is a perfectly unforeseen sentence, for in a former life I was afraid to cross the streets in my rural upstate New York town owing to my blindness and a corresponding insufficiency of imagination. The latter sounds hard but it's true: I didn't know, even in college, how I might live in the world. And though there are many answers to the puzzle one may call "how to live and what to do" in the end the only solution to fear (whether your life involves disability or something else) is love.)

Interpolation: walking is love; writing a circumstance of faith. So art can help you live but the atelier may smell like a water closet.

**

I'm improvident.

There are days when I feel the pull of the subconscious, little Kali with her necklace of skulls. "This is normal," I tell myself. Something delicate—a doll's chair breaks in my hand. "This is customary," I say. I feel like a man trapped in a tool shed, fingering the bolts and broken tools.

"Well," I tell my selves, "We Got It Bad, and That Ain't Good". How about a nice, cold glass of logical positivism?" Little Kali hates this. Nature doesn't Like the Romantic idealization of nature.

Etcetera.

**

Sometimes in the midst of people I'm so alone I ache. I also inflate balloons, throw voices, make up songs that only the most deliberate and obstinate children can enjoy.

**

"Memory is not an instrument for exploring the past but its theatre. It is the medium of past experience, as the ground is the medium in which dead cities lie interred."

—Walter Benjamin

(Helsinki: 1959)

Ruminant cold; clouds like machine parts, nothing fancy, a set of gears Low on the horizon, gulls walking sideways in the market square.

There were reindeer and old men and drunken sailors.

There were trolley cars filled with tough old Finns who had survived two wars with Russia and now retained entire dissertations on hunger in their heads.

Lights came on early. A darkness inside a darkness—weather "became" philosophy.

**

(Helsinki: 1999)

"Anxiety is the dizziness of freedom." (Kierkegaard)

The cold is numeric tension.

"Don't spoil my circles," said Archimedes.

I see a very old man making circles on the esplanade—looping circles built by oversized feet in the Finnish twilight.

"Nothing exists except atoms and empty space; everything else is opinion." (Democritus)

Look! A city of opinions!

Architectures of opinion!

But like Einstein, the snow does not believe in mathematics.

The city of my boyhood is a great polyhedron of shadows.

Winter in the far north is a miracle multiplied beyond necessity.

Leibniz wouldn't like it here.

Even the ravens of Helsinki know the unconscious arithmetic of winter.

This is not a conceit.

I once saw a raven standing in an empty baby carriage.

This was just outside a department store.

The raven was lifting one foot, then the other, carefully, as though composing a dance.

The mind is a question, asked of another question, the imperative, shadow asked of shadow.

When the parents came out with their baby the raven was gone.

**

Sometimes I see a child
See in him what I was like
And I want to say I'm sorry.

Jumping from place to place, and the dogs dancing with me.

Easy walking, late spring…

**

The shirt in my dream was from my childhood. It had dreadful stripes. I wore it in the hospital, a blind child, alone in a ward. The damned thing came back last night. You can count on the id.

**

(Helsinki: 1982)

It was a working-class bar and everyone was painfully drunk—that manly near death atavistic Viking hallucination of everything. After all these years so many wounds and so few praises. That was when a man I did not know turned to me and said: "You are a Jew!" "You're right," I said, because I was young and in love with poetry, "I am a Jew!" It was the first time I had ever felt the pins of anti-Semitism, I, a Lutheran with a long beard. He reached for me then but missed and grabbed another man. "You are a Jew!" he shouted. "No, it is I," I said, "I am the Jew!" But it was too late. They were on the floor and cursing, two men who had forgotten the oldest notion of them all: in Jewish history there are no coincidences.

**

Oh but how the words stink. "Shit on your whole mortifying, imaginary, and symbolic theater!" (Gilles DeLeuze)

I ask about beauty. One strives for it with the materials at hand. The black, high-flung vowels. The sprung intentions.

I need, like most writers, to keep a blank page in one room, the mind in another.

**

I wanted to be useful so I wrote a poem—
It was about Orpheus and his birds
So every bird was in it
All the birds in the world
And you know
It was not beautiful but terribly alive
Like a god who assumes a single shape
In sudden wind.

Autumn, or, Rain and a Lingering Soft Light of Sleep

I brew coffee while steam pipes talk
And my smallness in the scheme of things
Circles cat-like, though I have no cat.

**

Bride's dress, goat's wool, side by side in attic.

**

Here we walk now
My dead brother with me—
He's the one (sensibly) wearing
White rubber boots.

**

Pawnshop in Athens
Not far from Syntagma Sq.
Saw I'd remain half crazy
For one more day…

**

The trick:

There are lots of blind people my age
Who don't much like themselves.
Zig-zag lines of darkness
Make you (on the inside) drift like a leaf

**

Just a bone in a larger collection of bones,
What I am...call it the body if you like,
I know better. Soon now,
Rocks will roll straight through....

**

Mahler's Fifth.
Never got over it.
Seven years old.
Gramophone. Winter.

King worm drops to the floor having taken too much Beethoven. There are no loudspeakers in nature. At first he thrilled to the sensations— moisty guts buzzing with the string section, all that rum ti tum but then Ludwig nackered him with tympani and you know the poor bastard's just a worm who's lost. "How do you paint music?" he thinks, scooching his way on lemon-lime linoleum.

**

You breathed right up against the windowpane. Drew your mother from memory. Breathed again. She was gone.

**

Sometimes when I go to a funeral I'm aware the dead man knows my thoughts and there's no blinking it away. This is why I don't like ministers. They don't get this.

**

Everything I touched today belonged to Rimsky Korsakov.

**

Last night I sleepwalked to the river.
All rivers wear black coats days, evenings, doesn't matter.
Gave the river my white sleep shirt
Just to cheer it.
"You know," I said, "textiles…"

**

I have always hated the laughter of drunks. Their mirth is terrifying, like the sounds we've recorded from the sun.

**

The water shining through trees. Lake of childhood.
Long ago I saw despair on the surface.
Don't cry anymore!

**

King worm has a pair of wooden clogs which he uses as his winter and summer palaces. Wind blows darkness outside.

**

Do you ever see something innocent in the faces of old men and women? It's the pink undamaged. Always a miracle since mostly we're all ashes in rain.

**

I make mistakes over and over because I believe in assisting powerless human beings and animals. This means I argue with bureaucrats, sometimes noisily. The organizers don't like me much. I sit opposite them, at a big table, trying to see myself as an organ, a stomach in a larger body.

**

Missing the daily mail. Cutting open letters with a horse head knife.

**

Dogs know the heavens do not turn in silence and they're simultaneously cheerful.

**

Put on my little "peace hat" and pepper the aborning hour with words—names—Isaac Bashevis Singer, entelechy, sea cucumber, yellow mittens, Mother world. No one is about in my neighborhood. No one's awake. The houses are all buttoned, windows dark. My feet love the wet road. I think I need to pardon my youth. I hear the Phoebe bird. The age I live in has a dark taste. I'm seldom prone to this but I do sometimes wish I were a bird.

**

Count on me
Says the pea-stalk reindeer

**

Birches clouds books

**

"Embraceable You"—Bill Evans

**

Up and down the museum stairs above the physical museum. That's the ticket.

A Vague Love for Parsifal

1.

Yes. There's a suggestibility in books and last month when it was raining I read some mathematical calculations which were like various masks you'd find in a museum.

Straight off I wanted to be a Victorian mathematician with pencil and tablet; Macassar oil, inked hat, a vague love for Parsifal, a fascination with godforsaken places. These—from an old volume of algebra.

You wouldn't think you were suggestible. I am referring to myself. I'm confident I can remain half mad for one more day. It's the damned books that push affections and dissatisfactions—it's the books. All I want is flowers in the window.

2.

All right. A repeated fury has me by the toe. You see, the wind from dawn's hourglass opened my eyes and I wasn't ready. Now I want to tear the wreaths off my neighbor's doors.

There are so many unknown forces in the genes. Today I am a rabid king. Beware lest I appear in your yard. As Pablo Neruda once said: "Please, I beg a sage to tell me, where may I live in peace?"

3.

I'm listening to Beethoven's String Quartet #12 in E Flat, Op. 127.
How good on a dark day
To hear the strings

Like silver in a poor man's room
A clean force.
Quartet #12—
Afternoon
Before a trip
Darkness against my cheek.

4.

I bought an umbrella from a street vendor. The sky was clear. The weather report called for many days of sun. Sometimes you need a prop for the dark, unconscious side of life. I bought the thing for my dead mother. And then she was there with me on 8th St. And the crowd around us formed a dense black ant pile and the confusion all
about was indescribable.

5.

I fell out of a tree in 1955. Entered the world like a cicada. There's a chain of coffee places in New York City called "Pan Quotidien" which we are supposed to imagine means "customary bread"—but I generally hear it as "ordinary pain" which brings me back to the cicada. He walks around and then gets eaten. Once when I was in college I asked an entomologist why insect scholars aren't more philosophical. He said that science is exact. Which I still take to mean "being eaten is being eaten" and that's that.

You see, there's no meaning in being eaten. And across the street from "Pan Quotidien" is a Methodist church. For those who hope being eaten means something.

I fell out of a tree. Talk a lot. Make a clatter with my unsupportable wings. That's it.

6.

Birch branches curve slightly upward, less insistent than the oak. Across the street from me, in a different building, is a man who can explain why this is so, but we do not know each other.

Meantime, I guide my life by dreams, inefficient as always, prone to depression, occasionally putting my forehead down on the wet lawn early.

7.

I wonder if I can stick to one thought, like a small hunting dog? Riding the train to New York, looking at the spoiled factory towns, the haunted river, can I hold with one thought? I think I can be allowed a murmur. There has to be music in human silence.

There may be music after this. Shadows fall together in the tall grass of a railroad siding. Night crosses the desert of my understanding. I wonder if I can stick to one thought, like a small hunting dog?

8.

Topographers of the 18th century, here's snow with its rhymes and half words. I know how you put this on your maps. This is because I also try to avoid temporal distractions.

9.

How does it begin, the collapse of wish?
When you can't ask how it ends.
This is a joke of the rich
Who play chess with civic statues.

Notebook Elegy for Pentti Saarikoski

Today I sorted apples: for cider, for the horses, some for cooking...
I wrote lines in a notebook, "live for a time, after all..."

Nietzsche: "All truth is simple..."
Is that not doubly a lie?

Someone on the tram quotes Heraclitus,
The way up the way down...

**

Buddha:

"Chaos is inherent in all compounded things.
Strive on with diligence."

**

Pentti, here's Anselm: "each morning we're born again/of yesterday
nothing remains/what's left began today..."

Travelogue

I'm in Helsinki, a city where ever since childhood I've come and gone over the years. It's dark and rainy. I knew it would be. I love it. And yes, there's Sibelius playing in my head without an iPod, the stark and magnificent opening of "Finlandia" and I'm bundled in my black overcoat walking beside the sea. I love hearing strangers talk and laugh in steep weather.

**

It's important to know what you love especially the small things. I love the morning song from Peer Gynt, hot soup in winter, the sound of distant dogs barking at night, jazz piano any time.

Of course I love people, my wife, stepchildren, family, old friends, two horses in particular. But I talk about them all the time. I seldom say "I love that barn mouse."

**

T'was in Helsinki some thirty years ago I discovered the work of Bo Carpelan. He wrote lyric keyholes: "Join dreams together/to a single reality/a longing"

And so much longing there is. So much of it is outside the body and mind. It's in Lucretius' atoms. You smell it in the old book shops.

Horse, Man, Helsinki 1980

Early morning and only street sweepers and a lone policeman are in view. The cop is upright, descended from forest men and women. He's so bold he appears like a mythic extension of his horse, some god risen from an animal's back. I don't see well and have to draw near to find he's a horseman and when I'm very close I hear the man talking gently, so quietly he's like the ancient father we all long for, the horse father.

"My good girl," he says, "my creeper, my softly hooved…"

"Lord," I think, "he's James Joyce."

He says: "Girlie it's a pink-pink morning."

I'm walking home after a night of carousing.

"Your horse is beautiful," I say, peering upward.

In the world's darkest city they are tall and in love.

A Brief Poem Written at the End of a Bitter Year

What did they think at the edge of the world?
The type of thing written in poems…
One should say where money was useless.
The end of another year in a noisy country.
Where the poor have only flags of parody….
Where the crossbows failed.

Homage to James Tate

Master: I plucked my eyebrows, nervous,
Told my mother, "It's what I do" (how else
To explain Stukas
Straight to the eyes—
She wouldn't know from Stukas).
I'd have to explain
And it would be back to the shrink
Who'd ask me to draw pictures,
And in turn wouldn't know
Drawing when blind is poetry itself.

God at Home

All summer my fence was home to finches
Who didn't think of sagging boards.

They went about feeding
As decline held their feet.

I'm no carpenter. A poor steward
To pots, windows,

Letting things go is my work.
So I was no friend to the birds

Though I was inapparent, listening.

Micro Memoir 68

Dear Id: I've just now stepped off the train. I'm in tall weeds.

At the outer limits of phenomenology there's a terrible freedom. I adjust my soulful little eyeglass frames.

Conditions

Peaches ripened without help
My stepson said the moon followed him

One struggles to accept fences
My nature is not "of" the state

I can't play any kind of horn
You won't win by haunting others

My mirror sweeps the empty room
One day I'll be light on my feet

The picture fell and I couldn't mend it
My house leaned against my wishes

The Uproar of Living by Day and Dreaming by Night

Sometimes Beethoven makes my pulse race
Though I'm paring an apple
And the radio is in the next room.
Outside, rain, a neighborly fox
Nosing stiff winter grass.
Meanwhile my teeth wear out,
The brass buttons on father's uniform
Glitter in the attic.
Have I ever told you dear Ludwig...
A succession of immense birds....

Counting on My Fingers

No minister
At my father's grave—
I hadn't thought to ask—

His friends looked to me.
I recited Whitman:
A child asked
What is the grass.

With such intelligence
We rise alone.

PART THREE

Long ago
In the sun scorched meadows
With adolescence elongating into manhood
Life was like lemon on the tongue.
Then bitter again. Fresh. Bitter.
Do I know the difference any more?

——Lassi Numi

Elegy

People forget Odin spoke to the living and the dead.
They remember his raven only. Lie on the earth,
Press your face down by the roots,
Ignore the neighbors. This is Odin's day.
My mother and father dine in a garden
Where jonquils grow from broken vows
And Odin's verses are on the wind.

"Old Horse, What Is to Be Done?"

—for Robert Bly

I also want to live tonight
My pockets filled with ghost silver
The real coins I spent long ago
There are weeks, whole months
When I read only the ancients
I mean the dark one the river compulsive
A man who made clocks from string...
Time is a game played beautifully by children
Lately this is all I can think of
When I was very small I lived by a meadow
You loved me and I wasn't confused

Frost on Window Panes

I want to be unburdened, edge of town,
Twilight, the windows hereabouts
Yellow as the eyes of lions.
You can say what you like
But inference is faster
Than ethics, all those books
We read when young—
The good life, virtue, deeds
Ain't as fast
As the old heart
With its black napkin
Waving in my chest.
The bus passes the funeral home.
Tonight I'm half soul, half body.
I must be doing something right.

Larch, I'm Going Sad Like a Toy...

In an occupied land
I'm a doll-faced thing.
You can tell I was burned
For awhile. Don't
Fool yourself—
I got here by accident
Having believed too much
In others. How
Could they not
Fall in love with me—
And of course
They were simply
Running for their lives...

Meadow

I scatter my life across pages
Like no one else I know—
Among writers I'm lonesome.

Meantime I walk with the horses.
I want a good, hard, unpolitical cry.

Per Caputque Pedesqu...

Please dear book bring me consolation
Tall windows of hospitals can't do it
And the sunset is thin

Catullus: O this age! How tasteless and ill-bred it is!
Thanks old boy you're of little use

The darkness is knocking...

Underneath the Willow

If wings, if weather, if the cloudy dead
If potent as scripture
If lit like a match
If and if and the wall of forest
If the blue of sky
If you come home
If then, what we say
As if there was no if
If, the black candle we carry to bed

Blind, I Bought a Horse...

Blind, I bought a horse
Not to ride, though some would
My wife for instance—
No I bought him because
Of his loneliness

Orphic horse retired
From the track
Left standing in a stall

Have I mentioned his neck?
It's long as Noah's hope
For new sun—
Il miglior fabbro
I whispered
To the greater maker...

Hymn

Washing birds is the work of the gods
They've been at it some thirty thousand years
One may reasonably think
Birds were not clean
Before the gods came
I stand at a plate glass window
Drinking coffee from a paper cup
Many of my friends are gone
Leaves whirl under street lamps
Death's butterflies
I've a hymn in mind
Called *I Must be Home by Now*...

Late in the Day I Opened a Book of Shadows...

And I was not unhappy—
No one in my world
Could be found there
And I was not unhappy.
Sylvia Plath: "I thought
the most beautiful thing in the world
must be shadow."
Horace: "Pulvis et umbra sumus.
(We are but dust and shadow.)"
Auden of course:
"Every man carries with him through life
a mirror, as unique and impossible
to get rid of as his shadow."
And I was not unhappy...
Gilles Deleuze: "The shadow
escapes from the body
like an animal
we had been sheltering."
I was not unhappy...
Shakespeare—
"Some there be that shadow kiss;
Such have but a shadow's bliss."

Like a Falling Leaf...

The boy in me spins—
How to take him with me
As years advance?

Paavo Haavikko:
"I hear a happy tale, it makes me sad:
no-one will remember me for long."

The boy
Knew a thing or two.

He was never "in" time
Like those trees you see
In certain forests
Still green
Though there's true darkness
And we are long into September.

At the Arts Center

Sometimes I talk too much.
At other times I say nothing,
drink tea from a glass,
move books from one table to another.
All the rigamarole of art
Gets stuck in your throat—
So much to think about
In the moving world.
Schopenhauer's aphorism:
Man can do what he wills
But he cannot will what he wills.
A black river takes summer away
At the edge of a field.

Rain in a Tin Dish, Morning Cigarette...

At twenty, I'm anorexic, clear as can be—
Mother, a drunk, father up in air,
Mozart in hand, as much as I can get.
It's the no-one-loves-you minute,
So he adjusts his thick specs
Pays fierce attention
To birds he can't see.

Late in the Day

"—In late September many voices
Tell you you will die.
The leaf says it. That coolness.
All of them are right."

—*Robert Bly*

Under the apple trees shadows lengthen. It's a princely trouble I'm in—a problem from a thousand years ago. Something uncoils and I carry it into the house where it rests among my books. This presence, this siren is like a many armed figure of Durga waving her axe, riding a lion over a mound of skulls—but she's the smallest Durga in the world, small and green as the inch worm I discover scaling the *Collected Poems of Wallace Stevens*.

Fathoms down, under the waves, my long, informal apprenticeship.

Ode

What did it cost me to wake this morning?
My nation's history is a dark river.
If I am one of the saved, still swimming,
Who can I reach out to?
I do not want to be ashamed of the shore.

Alone in Any City

This is when the walls talk
And clocks fall backwards into histories
You know it and I know it
If you open a window
The curtains speak
Of provincial murders

Even on the driest days
One is saturated with fog and rain
Books help some
Philosophy is best
I had to deny knowledge
To make room for faith
Kant says—glad irony—

But in sad hotels
From Athens to Turku
Knick Knacks and carpets
Carry on filled with tears
In the countryside
Black grapes take light
Unwanted births go on
Small miracles are declared

Dear Jarkko

Now you're gone
I could transubstantiate

Become an ethereal megaphone
To tell and ask you things

As we did in Helsinki
Side by side

Bundled in raincoats
Scattered leaves flying

I said "dance"—
You said "death's butterflies"

We both saw the cruelty
Of money on faces

The solitary pride
Of businessmen

"The city is filled with hearts
That have been condemned

And torn down" I said
Quoting Neruda

You said "can't build suburbs
Fast enough"

It was fun being poets

Emergent God

—after Jarkko Laine

They speak of god along with cloud-esteem, sheep watching, plenty of softness. A few raise their glasses to the Michelin Man. Some open and close their hands. And sparks from the fire pop as the men drink grog. Night deepens. The walls of the tavern are warmer than the surrounding air. Outside its snow in May. A little psychiatrist with gold framed spectacles talks to himself about the altered situation which has now emerged.

A Brief Essay on Romanticism

All morning the restlessness of happening,
Greedy seconds, opera minutes
Until I want to beg the wind for a home.
We live in some nameless state
Falling continuously, falling
Illuminated and fitful.
Late winter, the earth
Smelling of mother darknesses
And I've no means to share this news
Save under the canopy of a poem
Where I'm writing very small.
Somewhere I think I might be burning.

After So Much Is Said and the Candles Are Low...

I'm no match for the godless nights
And if there are gods I'm no match for them either
I build a fence badly, tear it down after dark

**

I used to love Wallace Stevens
I was young

**

Thus the dog bursts into my poem
Follows me home

A mild wind follows the dog

**

Up river where a stand of birches leans
Walking with a spent candle in my coat

Lorca

Whose eyes are shot through with gold threads
Whose eyes are numbers—

Whose tongue steers songs of harvest knives.
There are many, too many to be sung.

He can be wheat at the end of summer,
Can be a wheel, his pulse

The revolutions
Of a long, clear night of love.

When September comes
He can be the first leaf in the fountain—

Perfect, death's butterfly...

To a Blind Man Selling Pencils: New York City

& then, others arrived:
Eyes first, surveyors, important men,
Men who wore the flag—runners
Who filled the streets in every town.
They carried sacks like thieves.
Every day such men feel their blood rise:
It uses them, returns them to the avenues
& I alone discovered them, one by one.
I was of the provinces. I was reflected
In their eyes like a fire.
Some men possess the color of origin—
The blind man is amaranth, a man-word of sorts,
A word that will be mistaken on earth.
Still I saluted the closed world
Without its consent,
Crossed the water of streets
And raised a sign
Unreadable as the moon.
My plea had the whiteness
Of things that have no use in life
And the words were nothing more than a scar
That someone must have given me.
Why then did your name appear
Like the marks of a wheel
In this unyielding light?

Questions to Answers

—*for Marvin Bell*

I was guilty of reversing things
So that water was sky when I rowed the boat early mornings
& I could see the purpose of trees was the perfection of earth—
Boyhood was like swallows in June, I flew everywhere
upside down & fast

O & I made solemn work of shadows
Begging the darkness
With my own darkness
A trick of the blind
Always the smallest grains of feeling

This is why the gravity of seasons
Holds me awake—
Almost foolish to say
I believe snowfall
Is the form and habit of gods
& they return against our will
& they talk of natural facts

They talk of natural facts...

Whenever I want to cry I think of boyhood and the gods...

The virtual emptiness of a child's early mornings blind in a boat...

Raven, Helsinki Harbor

—*for Meg Kearney*

The raven stood in a baby carriage and croaked to passersby. Her voice was a purple softness, really not much.

Something about a dingy bird is a question—where shall we work and live—or how did it come to this, a thing called "in public" standing near the ocean among balloons and pies?

Where did the baby vanish to?

A breeze rides in with its assignment. A woman laughs because she thinks she's partly immortal.

Leafage

Sometimes I cry aloud
Charon does also
It's hard work
Living moment to moment

**

Drama is crying with a script
I can't find mine
One definition of childhood

**

The old dog bit me

**

You can discuss Helen Keller
But you can't say what words
Perform on the inside

**

Have you seen a cormorant
Enter the sea?
That's my Helen Keller—
That falling....

**

I sat on the sofa where the former me had been so damned sad.

**

Greek myth, Boolean algebra, Lyell's hypothesis, Tu Fu—will they come with me?

**

"Leafage is hearsay when you're blind, until you hear it. Today is May 27." (Walking in a cemetery in Peterborough, New Hampshire.)

Ode to the Future Perfect

Mornings are when I'm happiest
So I hope to die around sunrise
There may be some book
A possible chariot
Some white gardenias
Or I might be out walking
With the last gods of summer
Behind me like stray dogs
Hoping I'll have something for them

Empty Paths

Don't sing to me about going down to the Crossroads—
Blind as I am, walking with a dog,
I'm always at lethal intersections.
These are countries without names.
The Devil has nothing to do with them.
Henry Ford sits on his cloud and points.

**

Read T.S. Eliot in youth.
Now when I go back
I riffle an album full of leaves.

**

After much is said and done
I made too many mistakes.
Entered strange parlors,
Uttered jokes in poor taste
Among people I didn't know.
Ate with the wrong utensils.

**

So he went a long way a long way:
Metaphorical luggage,
Regrets, coins, pocket comb,
Dharma in memory.
Broken thread dangling from his wrist.

**

Eliot:

"For last year's words belong to last year's language
And next year's words await another voice.
And to make an end is to make a beginning."

Oh but this isn't so.
The language stretches out.
On the bright side:
Language is a jacket you're not cold in.

**

So many times I've fallen asleep between two winds.
Even on this street corner.

Ripeness Is All

Beethoven's violin concerto is the perfect balance of milk and milk.
Adorno's dialectic is to body shame as money is to dialysis.
Disability studies is to ableism as crickets in August.
Wallace Stevens is to philosophy as bibles are to baking.
When poets have fun so do the tea cups.
Playing the violin burns about 170 calories per hour.

**

How close am I to becoming someone?
Of course I mean this in a moral sense.
I have the history of morals here in my cup.
Dregs of Aristotle.
Push them with my finger.
Happiness. Virtue. Work.
Remember to be a good flute player.

**

I ask so many questions.
Why do I believe I should soften death?

**

What is someone?
Is it cumulative flowers on a grave?
Even Shakespeare threw up his hands.
I joked once in a Helsinki pub:
Lear is a self-help book...
"Thou shouldst not have been old till thou hadst been wise."

**

Thank God I have the radio for company.
Thank God for William Shakespeare, life coach:
"And worse I may be yet: the worst is not
So long as we can say 'This is the worst.'"

**

After Ecclesiastes:

I haven't been true to myself lately
I press my face into barberry leaves
I weep among stems
If you know me you'll not be surprised
If you know me you too will be honest

Acknowledgments:

Several of these poems have appeared, sometimes in different versions, in the following journals. Grateful acknowledgement to the editors.

Red Wheelbarrow
Nine Mile
Seneca Review
Referential Magazine
Wordgathering

About the Author

STEPHEN KUUSISTO directs The Burton Blatt Institute's Programs in disability at Syracuse University where he holds a University Professorship. He is the author of the memoirs *Planet of the Blind* (a *New York Times* "Notable Book of the Year") and *Eavesdropping: A Memoir of Blindness and Listening,* and of the poetry collections *Only Bread, Only Light* and *Letters to Borges.* His newest memoir, *Have Dog, Will Travel: A Poet's Journey* is new from Simon & Schuster. A graduate of the Iowa Writer's Workshop and a Fulbright Scholar, he has taught at the University of Iowa, Hobart & William Smith Colleges, and The Ohio State University.

Kuusisto has served as an advisor to the Metropolitan Museum and the Museum of Modern Art in New York, and the National Endowment for the Arts in Washington DC, and has appeared on numerous television and radio programs including *The Oprah Winfrey Show; Dateline; All Things Considered; Morning Edition; Talk of the Nation; A&E;* and *Animal Planet.* His essays have appeared in *The New York Times; The Washington Post; Harper's; The Reader's Digest;* and his daily blog "Planet of the Blind" is read globally by people interested in disability and contemporary culture. He is a frequent speaker in the US and abroad. WWW.STEPHENKUUSISTO.COM

Colophon

The text of *Old Horse, What Is to Be Done* is set in Perpetua.
This trade edition was printed by BookMobile in Minneapolis, MN.

Publication of this book was made possible through the generous
contributions of the following donors:

Carol Biesemeyer

The Bishop Butler Society

Elinor Cramer

James Crenner

Eric Evans

Richard Foerster

Joshua Freedman

Judy Halley

David Hamilton

Grant Holcomb

Michael Jennings

Deena Linett

Lucy Michelson

Joseph Millar

Allison Moore

David Morris

Georgia Popoff

MORE POETRY FROM TIGER BARK PRESS

The Half-Life, by Roger Greenwald

Psychometry, by Georgia A. Popoff

I Play His Red Guitar, by Charles Coté

Per Diem, by David Weiss

Boy on a Doorstep, by Richard Foerster

Totem: America, by Debra Kang Dean

After Morning Rain, by Sam Hamill

Meditation Archipelago, by Tony Leuzzi

Fancy's Orphan, by George Drew

Translucent When Fired, by Deena Linett

Ask Again Later, by Nancy White

Pricking, by Jessica Cuello

Dinner with Emerson, by Wendy Mnookin

As Long As We Are Not Alone, by Israel Emiot,
translated by Leah Zazulyer

Be Quiet, by Kuno Raeber, translated by Stuart Friebert

Psalter, by Georgia A. Popoff

Slow Mountain Train, by Roger Greenwald

The Burning Door, by Tony Leuzzi

I've Come This Far to Say Hello: Poems Selected and New, by Kurt Brown

After That, by Kathleen Aguero

Crossing the Yellow River, trans. Sam Hamill

Night Garden, by Judith Harris

Time~Bound, by Kurt Brown

Sweet Weight, by Kate Lynn Hibbard

The Gate at Visby, by Deena Linett

River of Glass, by Ann McGovern

Inside Such Darkness, by Virginia Slachman

Transfiguration Begins at Home, by Estha Weiner

The Solvay Process, by Martin Walls

A Pilgrim into Silence, by Karen Swenson